COMBAT SPORTS

KICKBOXING

Clive Gifford

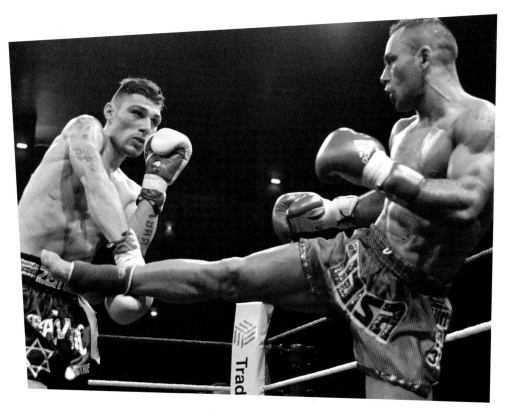

W
FRANKLIN WATTS
LONDON • SYDNEY

First published in 2008 by
Franklin Watts
338 Euston Road
London NW1 3BH

Franklin Watts Australia
Level 17/207 Kent Street
Sydney NSW 2000

Series editor: Adrian Cole
Art director: Jonathan Hair
Design: Big Blu
Cover design: Peter Scoulding
Picture research: Luped Picture Research

A CIP catalogue record for this book is available from the British Library.

ISBN: 978 0 7496 7880 7

Dewey Classification: 796.8

Acknowledgements:

20th Century Fox / The Kobal Collection: 4; Abdelhak Senna / AFP / Getty Images: 29; Adam Bailey / Action Plus: 20; Apichart Weerawong / AP / PA Photos: 14; Baa-Ram-Ewe / The Kobal Collection: 13; Bettmann / Corbis: 5, 7b; Franck Seguin / TempSport / Corbis: FRONT COVER, 21, 27; Henry Westheim Photography / Alamy: 9; Ingolf Pompe 6 / Alamy: 8; Interfoto Pressebildagentur / Alamy: 7t; Jason Dewey / Getty Images: 19; Jeff Spirer: 23, 26; Lara Jo Regan / Liaison / Getty Images: 12; Lionel Preau / DPPI Super Welters / Action Images: 1, 17t, 22; Liu Jin / AFP / Getty Images: 17b; Magali Girardin / AP / PA Photos: 11, 16; Nimatallah / akg-images: 6; Offside / L'Equipe: 18; Pedro Jorge Henriques Monteiro / Shutterstock: 10; Reuters / Corbis: 15; Santiago Ferrero / Reuters / Action Images: 24, 25; Fightingmaster.com: 28.
Every attempt has been made to clear copyright. Should there be any
inadvertent omission please apply to the publisher for rectification.

Printed in China

Franklin Watts is a division of Hachette Children's Books, an Hachette Livre UK company.
www.hachettelivre.co.uk

Please note: The Publishers strongly recommend seeking professional
advice and training before taking part in any contact sports. The Publishers
regret that they can accept no liability for any loss or injury sustained.

CONTENTS

WHAT IS KICKBOXING?

What do Hollywood celebrities John Cusack, Jessica Alba and Angelina Jolie have in common? Fast and furious kickboxing of course! The sport has developed from a number of other combat sports and is now practised and performed in countries all over the world.

This is a promotional poster for the film Fantastic Four. *Jessica Alba (top right) starred as Sue Storm.*

Boxing and much more

Kickboxing is a mixture of regular boxing punches and defence, combined with kicks and other moves from martial arts, including karate. Bouts are held in a ring; a square arena like that used for boxing matches.

★ SUPER-FAST FEET

American Bill Wallace (below) was a kickboxing pioneer who became famous for his lightning-fast kicking moves. During one kick, his left leg was timed travelling at a speed of over 90km/h!

Attack and defence

Many forms of modern kickboxing allow competitors to strike their opponents with four points of contact: their two feet and their two hands. Defence involves many techniques. These include bobbing – ducking your head to avoid blows – and weaving or moving from side to side. Blocks (see page 17) are used to stop an opponent from striking key target areas of the body, such as the head or stomach.

KICKBOXING ORIGINS

Modern kickboxing has its origins in countries all over the world, where different combat sports using hands and feet were first practised centuries ago. Three of the most important are pankration, savate and lethwei.

Pankration

The Olympic Games began in ancient Greece in 768 BCE. A savage new event, called the pankration, was introduced 120 years later. This was a no-holds barred combat sport. Competitors performed kicks, boxed and wrestled their opponent.

This sculpture from the late third century BCE shows two men in a pankration event.

Savate

Savate was a demonstration sport at the 1924 Olympics, and is the closest kickboxing has come to appearing at the modern Games. Savate developed from forms of street fighting in France, and also from fighting with feet carried out by French sailors. During the nineteenth century savate celebrities included the classical composer, Rossini, and the author of *The Three Musketeers*, Alexander Dumas.

This illustration of savate is from the 1900s.

SAVATE GLOVES

Many combat sports use different coloured belts to show a fighter's level of ability. Savate is different and uses gloves of different colours. There are blue, green, red, white, yellow and, for the very best, three levels of silver gloves.

Lethwei

Lethwei comes from the Asian country of Myanmar (formerly Burma) and is a tough and extreme combat sport. It is centuries old and allows kicks, punches, strikes with the elbows and knees and even head-butts. In the past, fights were held in sandpits. Now, fights tend to be held in boxing rings.

MUAY THAI

Muay Thai or Thai boxing is at least 800 years old. It has spread across the world from Thailand where it is the national sport. Muay Thai began as a form of hand-to-hand combat used by the Siamese army before Siam became Thailand. Acharn Tong Trithara opened the first US-based Muay Thai school in 1971.

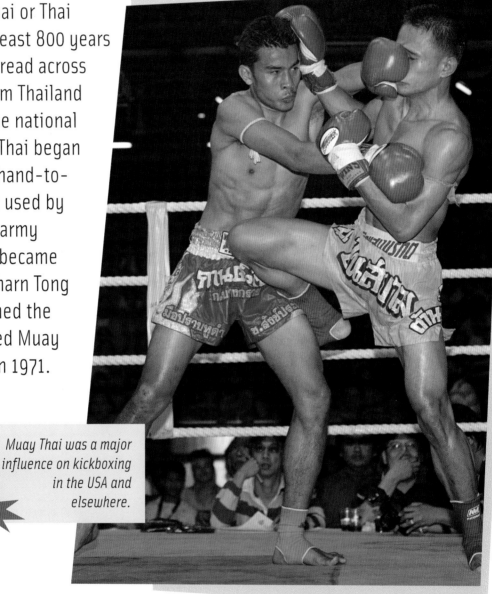

Muay Thai was a major influence on kickboxing in the USA and elsewhere.

Eight limbs

Muay Thai is known as 'the science of the eight limbs' because it uses not only the hands and feet but also the knees and elbows in attack. Apart from gloves on the hands, no protective clothing is worn. Many people think Muay Thai is the toughest of all kickboxing disciplines.

WAI KRU

A ceremony called *Wai Kru* occurs before a Muay Thai fight to honour each fighter's trainer. This often involves praying, facing the direction of their home, bowing and performing a series of dance-like movements. A trainer often places a ceremonial head band, called a *Mong Kon*, on the head of their fighter.

Muay Thai legend

Nai Khanom Tom was a Thai prisoner of war in 1774, but fought and beat 10 fighters from Burma to earn his freedom. The King of Burma was impressed and said, "Every part of the Thai is blessed with venom. Even with his bare hands, he can fell nine or ten opponents."

COMMON MUAY THAI TERMS

Bat – Block

Dtae – To kick

Dtoi Lom – Shadow boxing, literally to box with the wind or air

Gamagan – Referee

Gangkeng Muay – A competitor's shorts or trunks

Koo Ek – The main bout at an event. It literally means, 'number one pair'

Ram Muay – A dance performed as part of the ritual before a fight

Sangwien – The ropes surrounding a Muay Thai ring

Paa Pan Mue – Bandages worn under the gloves

Yaek – 'Break', a command used by a referee to separate fighters

Yang gan fan – A mouthguard

Yud – 'Stop', a command used by the referee

MODERN KICKBOXING

Modern kickboxing really took off in the West in the early 1970s. Many people involved in karate in the USA became frustrated with a lack of physical contact in their bouts. Some broke away from regular karate to develop kickboxing – then called 'full contact karate'.

SAFETY GEAR

In 1956, martial arts master Jhoon Rhee moved from Korea to the USA with just $47 in his pocket. During the 1970s, he invented padded safety equipment worn by kickboxers and other martial artists. His inventions helped boost kickboxing's popularity.

Today's kickboxers wear padded shinpads and footpads. Amateur kickboxers also wear padded headgear. Additional safety gear is worn for sparring (see page 20).

Getting organised

The first kickboxing organisation was actually called the Professional Karate Association (PKA). It was formed in the USA in 1974. It was followed by other organisations, such as WKAUSA and the International Kickboxing Federation (IKF). In 1975, a German called George Bruckner promoted kickboxing in Europe and helped form the WAKO – now short for the World Association of Kickboxing Organisations.

Kickboxing organisations help to regulate and arrange competition bouts.

ALL THE RAGE

In the late 1980s and 1990s, kickboxing became popular on a global scale. Thousands of gyms and clubs opened and the number of kickboxers rose into the millions. The sport became all the rage.

1989: the year of the movie

Kickboxing movies in the late 1980s helped raise the sport's profile. The most well-known are the 1989 films, *Say Anything*, *Kickboxer* (starring action hero, Jean Claude Van Damme) and the *Bloodfist* series. The eight *Bloodfist* films starred eleven-time World Champion kickboxer, Don 'The Dragon' Wilson.

Celebrity workout

One of the kickboxing performers in the first *Bloodfist* film was Billy Blanks. He had been the captain of the US karate team at the 1980 Olympics and became a personal trainer to stars, such as Paula Abdul.

Billy Blanks developed Tae Bo – an exercise system featuring some elements of kickboxing.

Twenty-first century kickboxing

Many combat console games feature kickboxing. The 2005 Playstation 2 game, *Tekken 5* featured kickboxing characters, such as Bryan Fury. A new wave of Asian films since 2000 has focused on kickboxing, including *Beautiful Boxer* – starring Muay Thai professional, Asanee Suwan, and *Ong-Bak* – featuring kickboxer, Tony Jaa. Jaa performed all his own stunts without CGI or stuntmen.

Tony Jaa's starring role in Ong-Bak *made him an instant kickboxing movie star.*

IN TRAINING

Training is the key to kickboxing success. Training can increase a kickboxer's strength and fitness, and also improve the speed and accuracy of his or her kickboxing skills.

Super stretch

Kickboxers need to be very flexible to twist, turn, dodge and raise their legs high to perform some of the kicking moves. They improve their flexibility by stretching their body's muscles for long periods at the start of a training session. This stretching also helps protect their body against injuries.

This kickboxer is stretching his leg before practising his kicks.

Hard graft

Training for top kickboxers can be ferocious. They work incredibly hard in the gym and perform conditioning exercises. They do these to boost their strength, speed and their stamina.

Many kickboxing students travel to Thailand to receive tough training.

'Train Hard, Fight Easy' is the motto of many champion kickboxers such as Kathy Long. She built her fitness and leg strength with running, known as roadwork. She says, "I believe the more conditioned fighter is going to win. I do a lot of various types of roadwork. An easy run is a five mile run up a mountain." Phew!

TOP 10 KICKBOXING MOVES 1–3

Kickboxing requires three major types of move – punches, blocks and kicks. Here are commonly-used examples of each type of move.

1 The jab

The jab is the most basic punch and the first a kickboxer learns. The jab helps keep an opponent at a distance and can be used straight to the head or angled down to strike the body. Kickboxers learn to step forward as they throw the jab in order to add extra power.

2 Punch and kick blocks

Blocks are a crucial part of defence. They are where part of the body is used to stop an opponent's attack by their fist or their foot. One classic block is to stop a kick to the body by pushing the opponent's foot away with your hand. This may leave the opponent open to your counter attack.

3 Jumping side kick

This is a great attacking move to use when an opponent has already been hit by another kick or a punch. The kickboxer jumps upwards and forwards and powers his leg forwards. He aims to strike the opponent's body firmly.

STRONG MIND, STRONG BODY

Kickboxing is not just about physical strength. It also places lots of demands on a fighter's mind. Kickboxers have to be mentally strong not only to think on their feet during a bout, but also to be positive and dedicated during their training.

Respect

Good kickboxers show people great respect inside and out of the ring. They don't trash talk (verbally abuse) their opponents. They never use their kickboxing skills to attack or intimidate people away from the gym. Most of all, a kickboxer should respect him or herself and avoid drugs and getting into trouble.

SUPER SAMIR

Frenchman, Samir Mohammed, takes part in World Kickboxing Network events. He says, "I will lose one day but of course I do everything possible to stay unbeaten so I never stop training. Every fight is a hard challenge as the one who will beat me will be famous in one fight." Samir is mentally tough, as is shown by his record of going 109 bouts without a loss!

Positive powers

To work hard in the gym and come back from losses in bouts, kickboxing coach, Eddie Cave believes kickboxers need to think positively. He urges students to not "dwell on negative thoughts or emotions, for they will produce negative effects in your life. Focus only on the positive results you would like to achieve."

Kickboxers train hard to strengthen their mind and body. They focus on one thing: performing at their best.

"Kickboxing taught me discipline. It taught me good sportsmanship. It gave me peace of mind. It was a great release of frustrations and anxieties." – *Benny Urquidez, kickboxer and coach, discussing the benefits of kickboxing.*

SPARRING

Sparring is a session where two kickboxers practise their moves on each other. Some beginners choose not to spar, but those who do, find it exciting and an excellent way to sharpen their kickboxing skills.

Spar class

Sparring should only be carried out with an experienced teacher or trainer in control of the sparring session. Extra safety equipment is worn including gumshields, which stop kickboxers losing teeth! Women may wear a chest protector whilst men wear a groin protector to stop painful low blows.

This kickboxing trainer is watching closely as two of his students spar with each other.

"Sparring should always be conducted [carried out] safely, without fear and with an open and questioning attitude." – *Pat O'Keefe, kickboxing trainer.*

Fighting stance

Kickboxers begin a sparring session in the fighting stance. This is similar to the stance used in boxing, with the feet shoulder-width apart and with the knees flexed. Their gloves are held up a small distance apart and up around face level.

Orthodox or southpaw

'Orthodox' or right-handed kickboxers have their left foot ahead of their right and their left hand up to eye level. Left-handed kickboxers are known as 'southpaw' and have their feet and hand position the other way around.

The kickboxer in the white shorts is standing in an orthodox stance.

TOP 10 KICKBOXING MOVES 4–7

Here are some more advanced moves used by kickboxers. These include the shovel hook – a short range, explosive punch – and three spectacular attacking moves that require great speed and timing.

4 Shovel hook

The shovel hook is used at close range to either the head or the body. With the fighter's elbow close to his body, he twists his hips and body round to land this curving punch from the side.

5 Axe kick

This is so named because the leg is raised really high and then chops down on an opponent's head or shoulders, like a falling axe. Kickboxers need masses of flexibility to perform this move.

6 Spinning back fist

A favourite of female kickboxing champions Kathy Long and Denise Taylor this is a power-packed punch where contact is made with the back of the hand. The boxer spins round sharply, pivoting on one foot, before extending an arm with a whip-like movement. The target is the opponent's jaw or forehead.

7 Spinning back kick

Spinning around on his front foot, the kickboxer turns his back on his opponent before releasing a powerful kick. He aims to strike his opponent's stomach with his heel.

COMPETITION KICKBOXING

Competition kickboxing contests between pairs of kickboxers usually take place inside a boxing-like ring or on a mat. Kickboxers try to win by scoring more points than their opponent – or by knocking out their opponent – within the time limit.

The WAKO Championship started in 1978 and is the longest-running kickboxing competition. This WAKO fight is between Michel Silveira (right) of Uruguay and Maurey Lionel of France.

Rounds and referees

Different competitions have different rules but kickboxing bouts tend to be explosive and short. They are often divided into two or three minute periods of action, called rounds, with a one minute break in between. A referee controls the fighters from inside the ring – they must follow his orders.

On target

Most kickboxing competitions feature three judges who sit on different sides of the ring. They mark fights, awarding points for accurate blows to allowed target areas (see below). Kickboxers can be disqualified and lose the bout if they ignore the referee, cheat or use illegal techniques, such as attacking their opponent on the ground.

Michel Silveira celebrates his World Championship win in the light-heavyweight category.

Semi-contact

Most kickboxers take part in amateur semi-contact kickboxing. This is where kicks and punches must only be aimed above the waist. Full protective clothing is worn in this type of kickboxing.

WAKO SEMI-CONTACT: POINTS SCORING

Punch – 1 pt

Kick to the body – 1 pt

Footsweep (if opponent's hands or body touch the ground as a result) – 1pt

Kick to head – 2 pts

Jumping kick to body – 2 pts

Jumping kick to head – 3 pts

TOP 10 KICKBOXING MOVES 8—10

The use of legs, knees and feet are crucial in kickboxing, but a single one rarely wins a bout. Kickboxers work really hard on combinations of two or more moves in training. According to kickboxing champ, Johnny Davies, "After you kick, your hands should be in a position to land strong punches as soon as your foot touches the floor. After you punch, your body should be in a position to throw a kick."

8 **Front kick**
For the basic front kick the kickboxer raises the knee of her front foot. She then thrusts the foot forward aiming usually for the middle of her opponent's body with the ball of her foot.

9 Outside foot sweep

Sweeps are allowed in some forms of kickboxing. For an outside foot sweep, a kickboxer slides his foot behind the bottom part of an opponent's front leg and sweeps it away. This can cause the opponent to lose balance, drop his arms and leave him open to punches or kicks.

10 Combination hook and roundhouse kick

This is a popular combination move. The strong hook punch is designed to open up the opponent. The kickboxer then spins round quickly on one foot and turns his hips and body into the roundhouse kick. The roundhouse kick is a favourite of many kickboxers, including Bill Wallace (see page 5).

FAMOUS KICKBOXERS

Kickboxing has already produced some legends of the sport. These champion competitors had to be extremely fit and skilful – with a massive desire to win.

Maurice Smith

Maurice Smith from the USA was one of the first superstars of kickboxing. He was crowned both WKA and ISKA Heavyweight World Champion and won 62 of his 75 professional kickboxing bouts. This included an incredible ten year spell when no one was able to defeat him.

Ramon Dekkers

A brilliant kickboxer from the Netherlands, Ramon Dekkers was the first person from outside Thailand to win Muay Thai 'Fighter of the Year'. He earned maximum respect for fighting Thai fighters in Thailand. His four epic battles with Coban Lookchaomaesaitong (two wins each) are remembered as some of the greatest ever Muay Thai contests.

Ramon Dekkers (left) in training.

Fikri Tijarti

Powerful Moroccan Fikri Tijarti was crowned WAKO World Champion in 2007 after defeating Spain's Mahy Cruz. An experienced veteran and three times European Champion, Fikri bases himself in the Netherlands along with his brother, Mourad who is also a kickboxer.

Fikri Tijarti with his WAKO World Championship belt after defeating Mahy Cruz of Spain.

Kathy Long

The USA's Kathy Long, nicknamed 'The Punisher', claimed a total of five World Championships, including the WKA World title. Her only loss throughout her kickboxing career occurred in 1990 against Britain's Lisa Howarth. She has acted in films and was Michelle Pfeiffer's stunt double in *Batman Returns*.

GLOSSARY

blocks
Defensive moves that stop an opponent's punches or kicks.

bout
A fighting contest between two people.

CGI
Abbreviation for 'computer generated image'.

combination
A series of punches and kicks thrown one after another.

focus pad
A foam-filled pad used to practise kicks and punches.

front kick
A kick where the foot is pushed straight out in front with toes up.

hook
A punch that swings around from the side in towards the opponent.

Muay Thai
Also known as Thai boxing, this is kickboxing where use of the knees, elbows and low kicks are allowed during a bout.

roundhouse kick
A powerful kick created by a circular movement.

shadow boxing (shadow sparring)
Fighting against a pretend opponent to improve a kickboxer's moves and stance.

side kick
A kick in which a fighter's lower torso is turned inward so that a heel lands on the target while the foot is parallel to the floor.

southpaw
A kickboxer who is left-handed. Southpaw kickboxers stand the other way round to right-handed kickboxers.

stamina
The ability to work hard for long periods.

stance
The standing position of a kickboxer.

Thai pads
A type of pad with straps fitted to a trainer's lower arm for students to practise their kickboxing moves.

FURTHER INFORMATION

BOOKS

There are lots of instructional books available on kickboxing. Check out your local library for books that suit you. The only way to really learn, though, is by joining kickboxing classes at a gym or club.

Kickboxing

Pat O'Keefe (Skyhorse Publishing, 2007)
Written by a British team coach, this book is for serious kickboxers with technique drills, pointers and a full training programme.

Kick Boxing

Eddie Cave (New Holland Pub. Ltd, 2001)
A colourful guide to kickboxing.

Diary of A Kickboxing Freak

Clive Gifford (Heinemann, 2004)
A guide to the sport through the eyes of a teenager who progresses from total beginner to aspiring champion.

DVDs AND MOVIES

Some of these movies are not suitable for all ages:

The Chris Kent Kickboxing Course DVD

For beginners, this shows the basics of kickboxing from warming up to sparring, bag work and basic moves.

Essential Kickboxing – Vol. 1 – Offensive Techniques (Summersdale Productions, 2006)

Short run-time but packed with technique tips on performing attacking moves.

Ong-Bak – The Thai Warrior

(Prachya Pinkaew, 2003)
Superb, all-action movie starring kickboxer, Tony Jaa.

Kings Of Muay Thai Boxing – Vol. 1

(Kickboxing Films, 2001)
Footage from great Muay Thai bouts of the 1980s and 1990s, featuring legends in action including Coban Lookchaomaesaitong and Ramon Dekkers.

WEBSITES

www.wka.co.uk

The World Kickboxing Association's website contains lists of clubs, rankings and news of upcoming events.

www.wkausa.com

The official website of the World Kickboxing Association, USA. This site contains details of rules for both amateur and professional kickboxers, as well as training information and future tournaments and events.

www.diamonddekkers.com

Official website of legendary kickboxer and Muay Thai fighter, Ramon 'Diamond' Dekkers.

www.ikfkickboxing.com

The International Kickboxing Federation's website. This site has masses of information on rules, training, events and its past champions.

www.worldkickboxingnetwork.com

Home on the internet of the World Kickboxing Network, an organisation that promotes bouts and events.

INDEX